LITTLE WHISPERS OF WISDOM

FOR BUSY WOMEN

W9-APJ-013

ISBN 978-1-60260-373-8

Published by Barbour Publishing, Inc., P.O. Box 719, Uhrichsville, Ohio 44683, www.barbourbooks.com

Our mission is to publish and distribute inspirational products offering exceptional value and biblical encouragement to the masses.

Printed in China.

LITTLE WHISPERS OF WISDOM

FOR BUSY WOMEN

BARBOUR
PUBLISHING

Joy is prayer. Joy is strength. Joy is love.
Joy is a net of love by which
you can catch souls.

MOTHER TERESA

Look at a day when you are supremely satisfied at the end. It is not a day when you lounge around doing nothing; it is when you have had everything to do, and you have done it.

MARGARET THATCHER

*Seize this day, and put the
least possible trust in tomorrow.*

HORACE

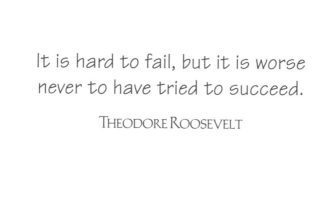

It is hard to fail, but it is worse
never to have tried to succeed.

THEODORE ROOSEVELT

*The great recipe for success
is to work and always work.*

LEON GAMBETTA

Consider the lilies how they grow.

LUKE 12:27 KJV

I have faith that yields to none.

OVID

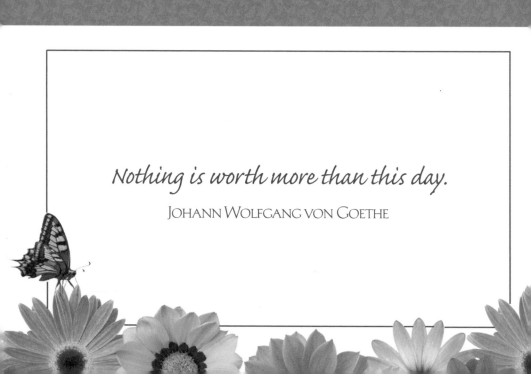

Nothing is worth more than this day.

JOHANN WOLFGANG VON GOETHE

You have achieved success if you have lived well, laughed often, and loved much.

ANONYMOUS

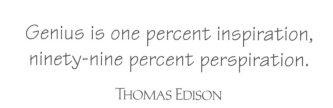

Genius is one percent inspiration,
ninety-nine percent perspiration.

THOMAS EDISON

Trust God to move mountains,
but keep on digging.

OUR DAILY BREAD

Who stops being better stops being good.

OLIVER CROMWELL

I cannot change the whole world,
but I can change a small part of it.

KAY FLORENTINO

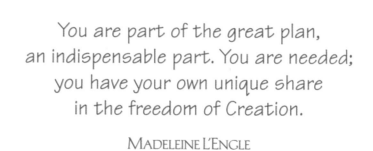

You are part of the great plan,
an indispensable part. You are needed;
you have your own unique share
in the freedom of Creation.

MADELEINE L'ENGLE

Do not wait to strike till the iron is hot;
but make it hot by striking.

WILLIAM B. SPRAGUE

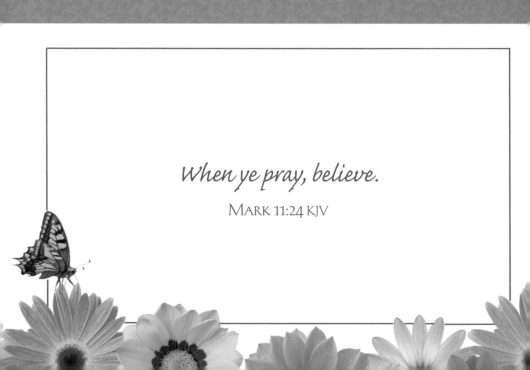

When ye pray, believe.

MARK 11:24 KJV

What you achieve through the journey of life
is not as important as who you become.

UNKNOWN

We are what we repeatedly do. Excellence, therefore, is not an act but a habit.

ARISTOTLE

*Never let the fear of striking
out get in your way.*

GEORGE HERMAN "BABE" RUTH

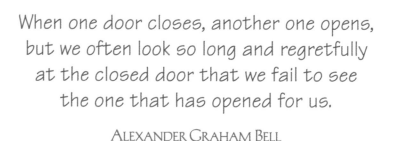

When one door closes, another one opens,
but we often look so long and regretfully
at the closed door that we fail to see
the one that has opened for us.

ALEXANDER GRAHAM BELL

The greatest gift we can give one another is rapt attention to one another's existence.

SUE ATCHLEY EBAUGH

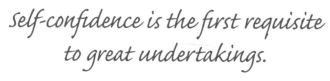

*Self-confidence is the first requisite
to great undertakings.*

SAMUEL JOHNSON

Do not let trifles disturb your tranquility of mind. . . . Life is too precious to be sacrificed for the nonessential and transient. . . . Ignore the inconsequential.

GRENVILLE KLEISER

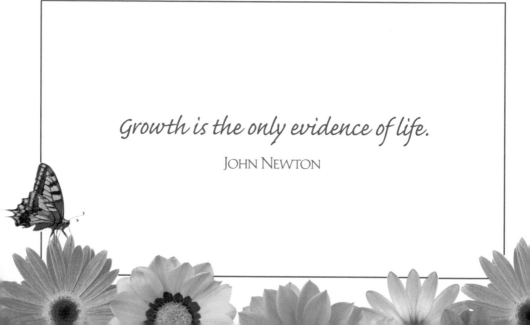

Growth is the only evidence of life.

JOHN NEWTON

Real joy comes not from ease or
riches or from the praise of men,
but from doing something worthwhile.

SIR WILFRED GRENFELL

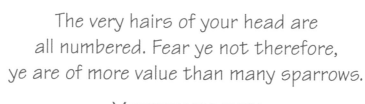

The very hairs of your head are
all numbered. Fear ye not therefore,
ye are of more value than many sparrows.

MATTHEW 10:30–31 KJV

Experience teaches only the teachable.

ALDOUS HUXLEY

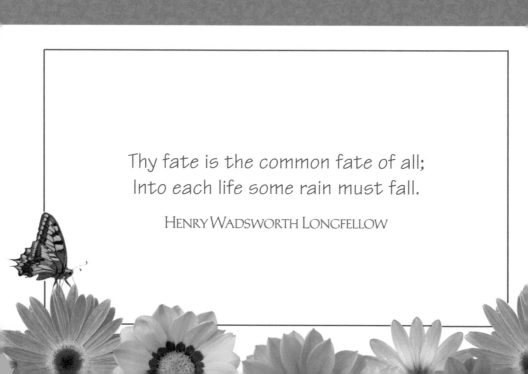

Thy fate is the common fate of all;
Into each life some rain must fall.

HENRY WADSWORTH LONGFELLOW

*Courage is the ladder on which
all the other virtues mount.*

CLARE BOOTH LUCE

Leap, and the net will appear.

UNKNOWN

I cannot give you the formula for success, but I can give you the formula for failure— which is: Try to please everybody.

HERBERT B. SWOPE

*The man who has confidence in himself
gains the confidence of others.*

HASIDIC SAYING

Little faith will bring your soul to heaven,
but great faith will bring heaven to your soul.

CHARLES H. SPURGEON

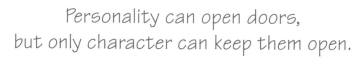

Personality can open doors,
but only character can keep them open.

ELMER G. LETTERMAN

*Experience is the mother of truth;
and by experience we learn wisdom.*

WILLIAM SHIPPEN JR.

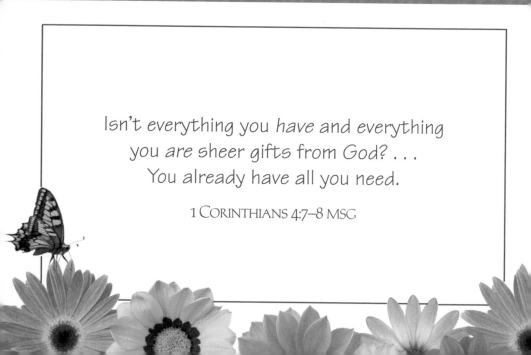

Isn't everything you *have* and everything
you *are* sheer gifts from God? . . .
You already have all you need.

1 CORINTHIANS 4:7–8 MSG

People grow through experience if they meet life honestly and courageously. This is how character is built.

ELEANOR ROOSEVELT

Let us have faith that right makes might.

ABRAHAM LINCOLN

The greatest satisfaction in life is
achieving what everyone said could not be done.

CHINESE PROVERB

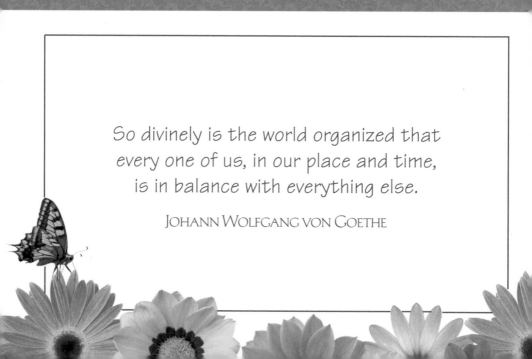

So divinely is the world organized that
every one of us, in our place and time,
is in balance with everything else.

JOHANN WOLFGANG VON GOETHE

I do not pray for success; I ask for faithfulness.

MOTHER TERESA

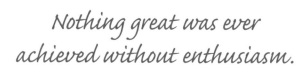

*Nothing great was ever
achieved without enthusiasm.*

RALPH WALDO EMERSON

The reason some [people] do not succeed
is because their wishbone is where
their backbone ought to be.

ANONYMOUS

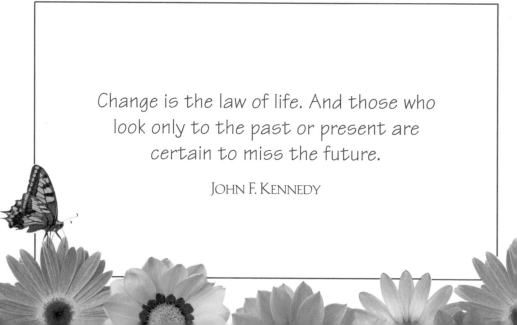

Change is the law of life. And those who
look only to the past or present are
certain to miss the future.

JOHN F. KENNEDY

*I am not afraid of tomorrow, for I have
seen yesterday, and I love today.*

WILLIAM ALLEN WHITE

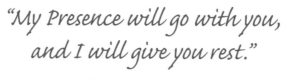

"My Presence will go with you,
and I will give you rest."

EXODUS 33:14 NIV

You see things; and you say "Why?"
But I dream things that never were;
and I say "Why not?"

GEORGE BERNARD SHAW

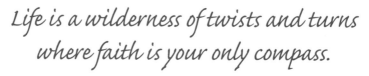

Life is a wilderness of twists and turns where faith is your only compass.

PAUL SANTAGUIDA

Yesterday is gone. Tomorrow has not yet come.
We have only today. Let us begin.

MOTHER TERESA

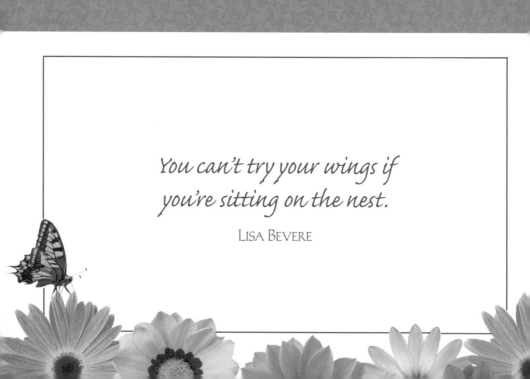

You can't try your wings if you're sitting on the nest.

LISA BEVERE

Take the first step in faith.
You don't have to see the whole staircase—
just take the first step.

MARTIN LUTHER KING JR.

Love comforteth like sunshine after rain.

WILLIAM SHAKESPEARE

Within our dreams and aspirations
we find our opportunities.

SUE ATCHLEY EBAUGH

It is a mistaken idea that greatness and great success mean the same thing.

ANONYMOUS

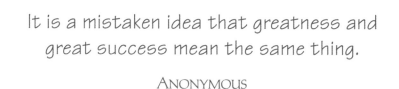

What I must do is all that concerns me,
not what the people think.

RALPH WALDO EMERSON

Mercy, peace and love be yours in abundance.

JUDE 1:2 NIV

The future belongs to those who believe
in the beauty of their dreams.

UNKNOWN

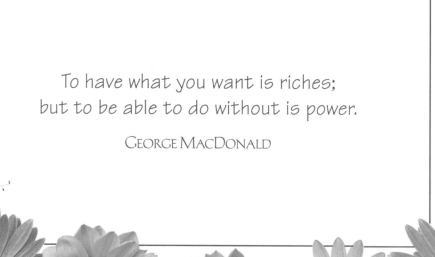

To have what you want is riches;
but to be able to do without is power.

GEORGE MACDONALD

*Choose always the way that seems best,
however rough it may be.*

PYTHAGORAS

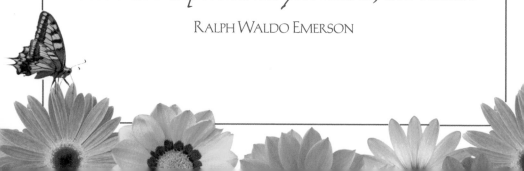

All life is an experiment.
The more experiments you make, the better.

RALPH WALDO EMERSON

Simplicity is indeed often the sign
of truth and a criterion of beauty.

MAHLON HOAGLAND

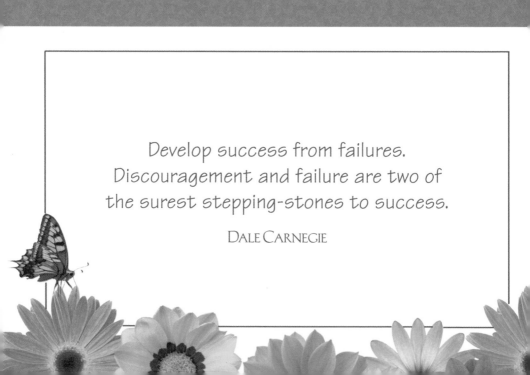

Develop success from failures.
Discouragement and failure are two of
the surest stepping-stones to success.

DALE CARNEGIE

Great works are performed not by strength but by perseverance.

SAMUEL JOHNSON

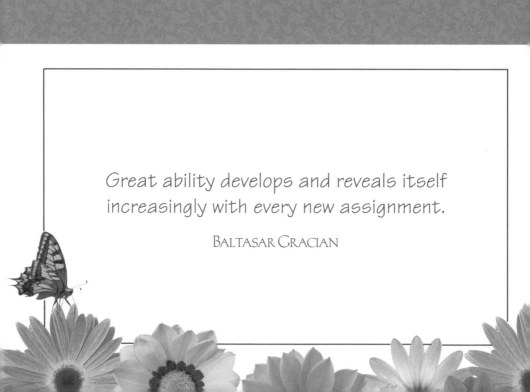

Great ability develops and reveals itself
increasingly with every new assignment.

BALTASAR GRACIAN

The world of tomorrow belongs to the person who has the vision today.

ROBERT SCHULLER

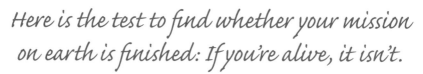

Here is the test to find whether your mission
on earth is finished: If you're alive, it isn't.

RICHARD BACH

Prepare your minds for action; be self-controlled;
set your hope fully on the grace to be given
you when Jesus Christ is revealed.

1 PETER 1:13 NIV

There are only two ways to live your life.
One is as though nothing is a miracle.
The other is as though everything is a miracle.

ALBERT EINSTEIN

But if I knew everything, there would be no wonder, because what I believe is far more than I know.

MADELEINE L'ENGLE

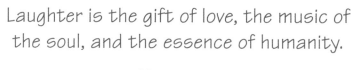

Laughter is the gift of love, the music of the soul, and the essence of humanity.

UNKNOWN

Success is getting what you want.
Happiness is wanting what you get.

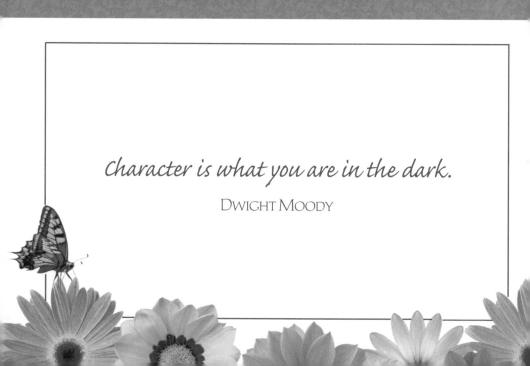

Character is what you are in the dark.

<small>DWIGHT MOODY</small>

The only reward of virtue is virtue;
the only way to have a friend is to be one.

RALPH WALDO EMERSON

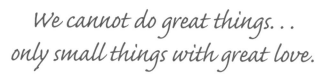

We cannot do great things. . .
only small things with great love.

MOTHER TERESA

It is only with the heart that one can see rightly.
What is essential is invisible to the eye.

ANTOINE DE SAINT-EXUPÉRY

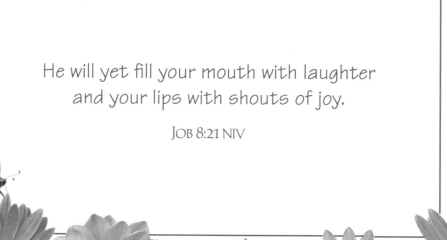

He will yet fill your mouth with laughter
and your lips with shouts of joy.

JOB 8:21 NIV

*All along life's broad highway
I found loveliness today.*

CARLETON EVERETT KNOX

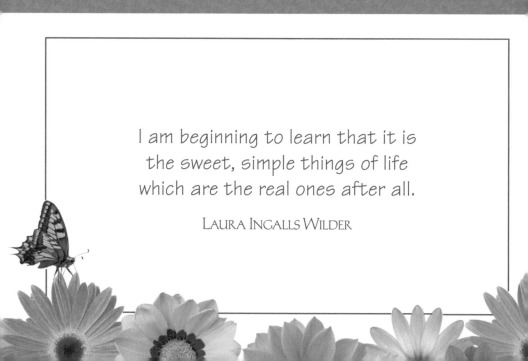

I am beginning to learn that it is
the sweet, simple things of life
which are the real ones after all.

LAURA INGALLS WILDER

Never be afraid to trust an unknown future to a known God.

CORRIE TEN BOOM

Keep your friendships in repair.

RALPH WALDO EMERSON

To see a world in a grain of sand
And a heaven in a wild flower,
Hold infinity in the palm of your hand
And eternity in an hour.

WILLIAM BLAKE

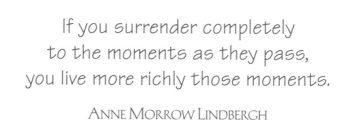

If you surrender completely
to the moments as they pass,
you live more richly those moments.

ANNE MORROW LINDBERGH

Love is love's reward.

JOHN DRYDEN

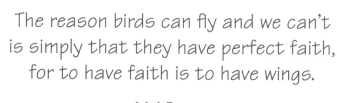

The reason birds can fly and we can't
is simply that they have perfect faith,
for to have faith is to have wings.

J. M. BARRIE

Shoot for the moon. Even if you miss,
you'll land among the stars.

LES BROWN

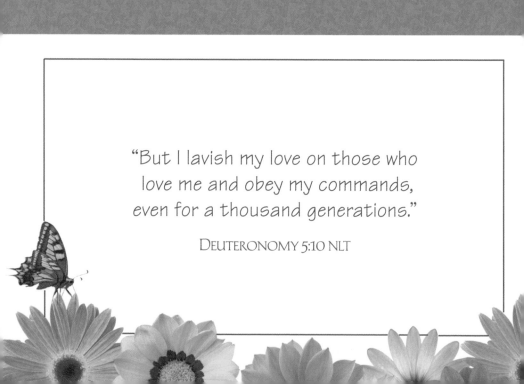

"But I lavish my love on those who love me and obey my commands, even for a thousand generations."

DEUTERONOMY 5:10 NLT

If you can imagine it, you can achieve it.
If you can dream it, you can become it.

WILLIAM ARTHUR WARD

Respect is love in plain clothes.

FRANKIE BYRNE

Look at life through the windshield,
not the rearview mirror.

BYRD BAGGETT

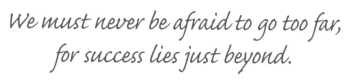

We must never be afraid to go too far,
for success lies just beyond.

MARCEL PROUST

Write it on your heart that every day
is the best day in the year.

RALPH WALDO EMERSON

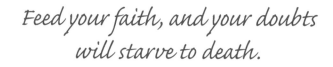

Feed your faith, and your doubts
will starve to death.

OUR DAILY BREAD

Whoever is happy will make others happy, too.
He who has courage and faith
will never perish in misery.

ANNE FRANK

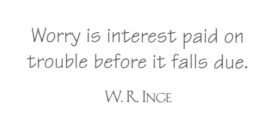

Worry is interest paid on
trouble before it falls due.

W. R. Inge

The seed of joy grows best in a field of peace.

ROBERT J. WICKS

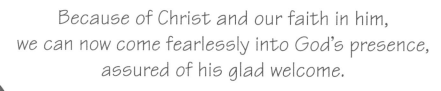

Because of Christ and our faith in him,
we can now come fearlessly into God's presence,
assured of his glad welcome.

EPHESIANS 3:12 NLT

Life is a series of surprises.

RALPH WALDO EMERSON

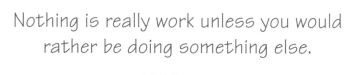

Nothing is really work unless you would
rather be doing something else.

J. M. BARRIE

Life is either a daring adventure or nothing.

HELEN KELLER

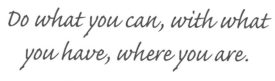

*Do what you can, with what
you have, where you are.*

THEODORE ROOSEVELT

Innocence is like polished armor;
it adorns and defends.

BISHOP ROBERT SOUTH

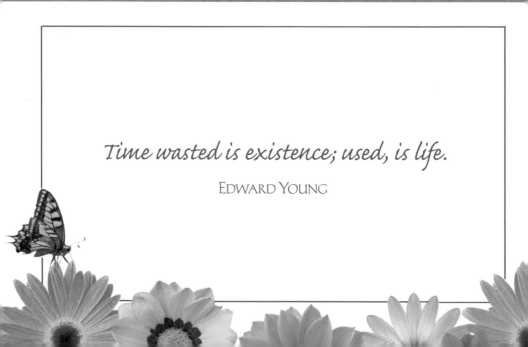

Time wasted is existence; used, is life.

EDWARD YOUNG

It is better to have nobility of
character than nobility of birth.

JEWISH PROVERB

The things we think on are the things that feed our souls. If we think on pure and lovely things, we shall grow pure and lovely like them.

HANNAH WHITALL SMITH

Experience is a jewel.

WILLIAM SHAKESPEARE

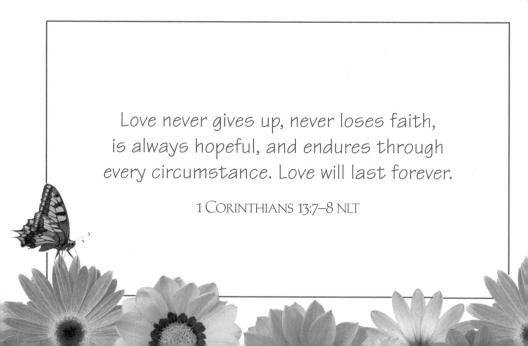

Love never gives up, never loses faith,
is always hopeful, and endures through
every circumstance. Love will last forever.

1 CORINTHIANS 13:7–8 NLT

*To love abundantly is to live abundantly,
and to love forever is to live forever.*

ANONYMOUS

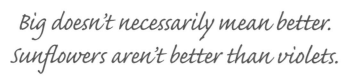

Big doesn't necessarily mean better.
Sunflowers aren't better than violets.

EDNA FERBER

Your thoughts are building your life—hourly, daily. Your thoughts are what your destiny is.

UNKNOWN

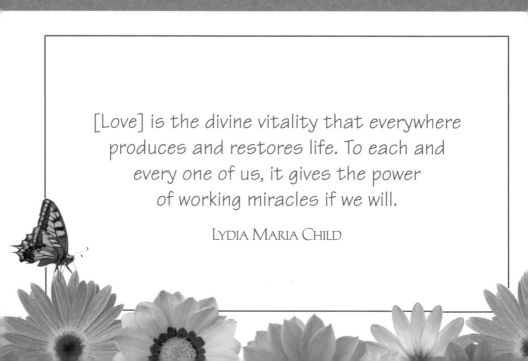

[Love] is the divine vitality that everywhere
produces and restores life. To each and
every one of us, it gives the power
of working miracles if we will.

LYDIA MARIA CHILD

I have learned to live each day as it comes and not to borrow trouble by dreading tomorrow.

Dorothy Dix

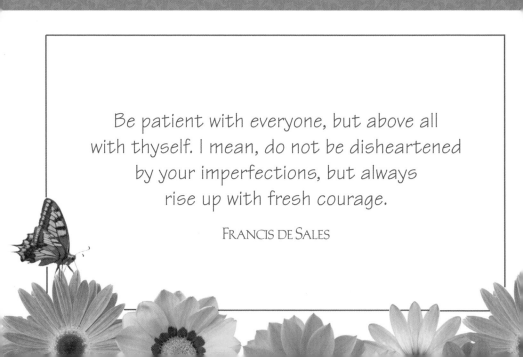

Be patient with everyone, but above all
with thyself. I mean, do not be disheartened
by your imperfections, but always
rise up with fresh courage.

FRANCIS DE SALES

Anybody can sympathize with the sufferings of a friend, but it requires a very fine nature to sympathize with a friend's success.

OSCAR WILDE

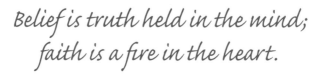

Belief is truth held in the mind;
faith is a fire in the heart.

JOSEPH FORT NEWTON

Yes, you can be a dreamer and a doer,
too, if you will remove one word
from your vocabulary: impossible.

ROBERT SCHULLER

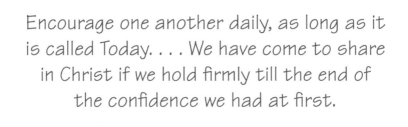

Encourage one another daily, as long as it is called Today. . . . We have come to share in Christ if we hold firmly till the end of the confidence we had at first.

HEBREWS 3:13–14 NIV

While our hearts are pure,
our lives are happy and our peace is sure.

WILLIAM WINTER

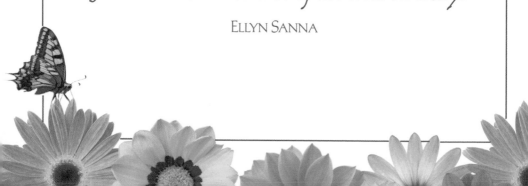

God alone is the source of all true serenity.

ELLYN SANNA

The best and most beautiful things in
the world cannot be seen or even touched.
They must be felt with the heart.

HELEN KELLER

Friendship is one of the sweetest joys of life.
Many might have failed beneath the bitterness
of their trial had they not found a friend.

CHARLES SPURGEON

There are two ways of spreading light: to be the candles or the mirror that reflects it.

EDITH WHARTON

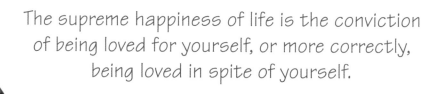

The supreme happiness of life is the conviction of being loved for yourself, or more correctly, being loved in spite of yourself.

VICTOR HUGO

We are all pencils in the hand of a writing God, who is sending love letters to the world.

MOTHER TERESA

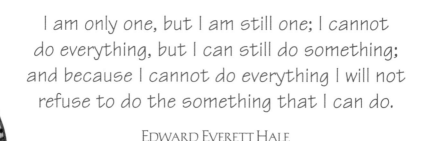

I am only one, but I am still one; I cannot
do everything, but I can still do something;
and because I cannot do everything I will not
refuse to do the something that I can do.

EDWARD EVERETT HALE

Trouble shared is trouble halved.

DOROTHY SAYERS

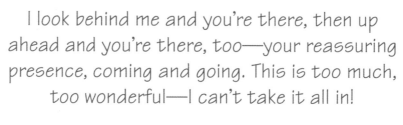

I look behind me and you're there, then up ahead and you're there, too—your reassuring presence, coming and going. This is too much, too wonderful—I can't take it all in!

PSALM 139:5–6 MSG

Angels fly because they take themselves lightly.

UNKNOWN

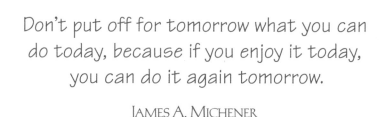

Don't put off for tomorrow what you can
do today, because if you enjoy it today,
you can do it again tomorrow.

JAMES A. MICHENER

We find in life exactly what we put into it.

RALPH WALDO EMERSON

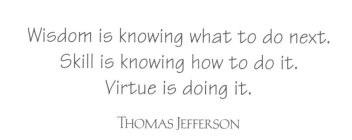

Wisdom is knowing what to do next.
Skill is knowing how to do it.
Virtue is doing it.

THOMAS JEFFERSON

*Goodness is the only investment
that never fails.*

HENRY DAVID THOREAU

Work first, then rest.

JOHN RUSKIN

What lies behind us and what lies before us are tiny matters compared to what lies within us.

RALPH WALDO EMERSON

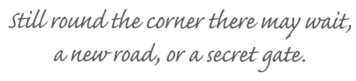

Still round the corner there may wait,
a new road, or a secret gate.

J. R. R. TOLKIEN

Our greatest glory consists not in never falling,
but in rising every time we fall.

Oliver Goldsmith

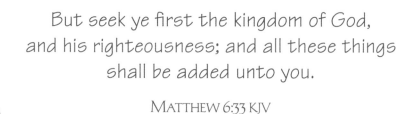

But seek ye first the kingdom of God,
and his righteousness; and all these things
shall be added unto you.

MATTHEW 6:33 KJV

To have joy one must share it—
happiness was born a twin.

LORD BYRON

Love is, above all, the gift of oneself.

JEAN ANOUILH

The future is something which everyone
reaches at the rate of sixty minutes an hour,
whatever he does, whoever he is.

C. S. LEWIS

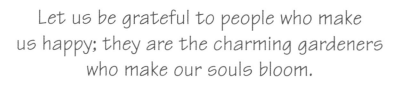

Let us be grateful to people who make
us happy; they are the charming gardeners
who make our souls bloom.

MARCEL PROUST

When doubts come, meet them, not with arguments, but with assertions of faith.

HANNAH WHITALL SMITH

God has given us two hands—one to receive with and the other to give with. We are not cisterns made for hoarding; we are channels made for sharing.

BILLY GRAHAM

Luck marches with those
who give their very best.

H. JACKSON BROWN JR.

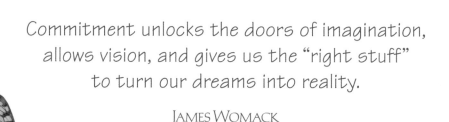

Commitment unlocks the doors of imagination,
allows vision, and gives us the "right stuff"
to turn our dreams into reality.

JAMES WOMACK

We aim high above the mark to hit the mark.

RALPH WALDO EMERSON

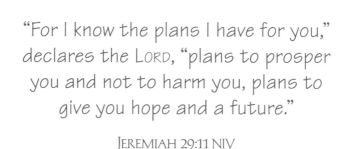

"For I know the plans I have for you," declares the LORD, "plans to prosper you and not to harm you, plans to give you hope and a future."

JEREMIAH 29:11 NIV

Hope springs exulting on triumphant wings.

ROBERT BURNS

Hand grasps hand, eye lights eye. . .
And great hearts expand, and grow.

ROBERT BROWNING

Resolve to see the world on the
sunny side, and you have almost won
the battle of life at the outset.

SIR ROGER L'ESTRANGE

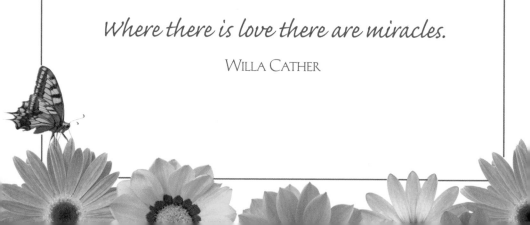

Where there is love there are miracles.

WILLA CATHER

Each dawn holds a new hope
for a new plan, making the start
of each day the start of a new life.

GINA BLAIR

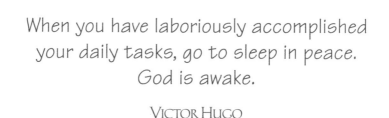

When you have laboriously accomplished
your daily tasks, go to sleep in peace.
God is awake.

VICTOR HUGO

*When I am delivering my very best,
that is when I feel successful.*

ART FETTIG

Hide not your talents.
They for use were made.
What's a sundial in the shade?

BENJAMIN FRANKLIN

By perseverance, the snail reached the ark.

CHARLES SPURGEON

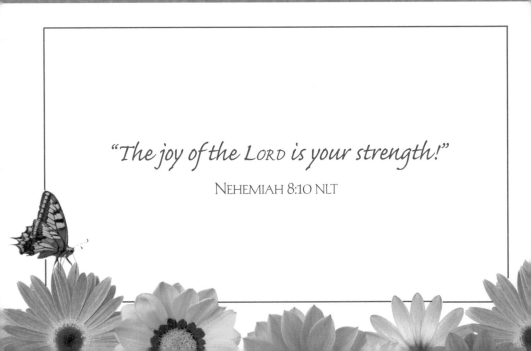

"*The joy of the LORD is your strength!*"

NEHEMIAH 8:10 NLT

Success seems to be largely a matter
of hanging on after others have let go.

WILLIAM FEATHER

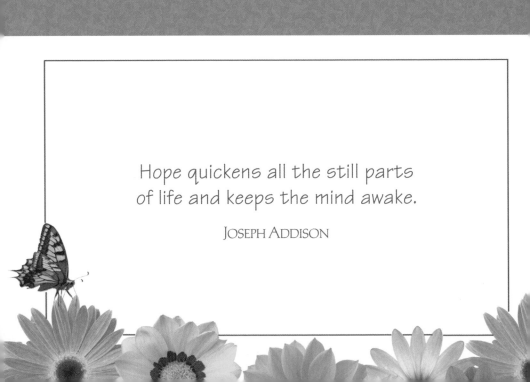

Hope quickens all the still parts
of life and keeps the mind awake.

JOSEPH ADDISON

Courage is the capacity to go ahead in spite of the fear.

SCOTT PECK

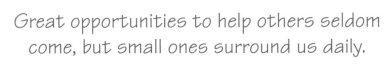

Great opportunities to help others seldom
come, but small ones surround us daily.

SALLY KOCH

A loving heart is the truest wisdom.

CHARLES DICKENS

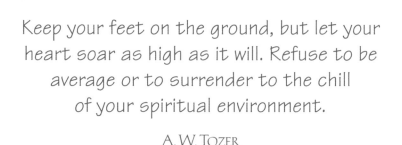

Keep your feet on the ground, but let your heart soar as high as it will. Refuse to be average or to surrender to the chill of your spiritual environment.

A. W. TOZER

To live is so startling it leaves little time for anything else.

EMILY DICKINSON

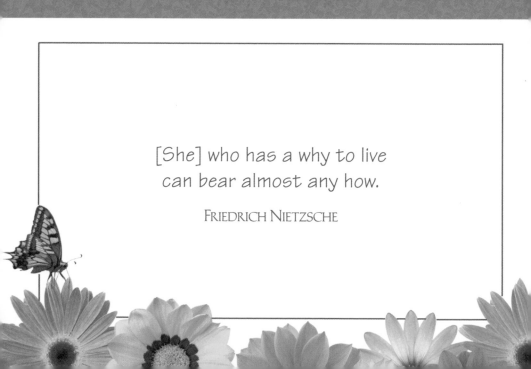

[She] who has a why to live
can bear almost any how.

FRIEDRICH NIETZSCHE

The secret to success is to do the common things uncommonly well.

JOHN D. ROCKEFELLER JR.

May the God of hope fill you will all joy and peace as you trust in him, so that you may overflow with hope by the power of the Holy Spirit.

ROMANS 15:13 NIV

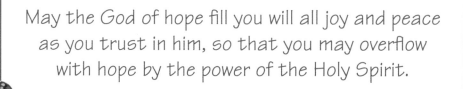

No act of kindness, no matter how small, is ever wasted.

AESOP

I have a simple philosophy: Fill what's empty.
Empty what's full. Scratch where it itches.

ALICE ROOSEVELT LONGWORTH

The great use of life is to spend it for something that will outlast it.

WILLIAM JAMES

What joy is better than the news of friends?

ROBERT BROWNING

In three words I can sum up everything
I've learned about life: it goes on.

ROBERT FROST

They can conquer who believe they can.

RALPH WALDO EMERSON

Your happiness comes from within you,
not from the money you make, the trips
you take, or the things you own.

FAITH STEWART

It is not length of life, but depth of life.

RALPH WALDO EMERSON

You will find, as you look back upon your life,
that the moments when you have really lived
are the moments when you have done
things in the spirit of love.

HENRY DRUMMOND

God is able to make all grace abound to you, so that in all things at all times, having all that you need, you will abound in every good work.

2 CORINTHIANS 9:8 NIV

Life is change. Growth is optional.
Choose wisely.

KAREN KAISER

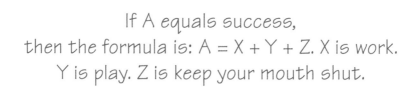

If A equals success,
then the formula is: A = X + Y + Z. X is work.
Y is play. Z is keep your mouth shut.

ALBERT EINSTEIN